MINDSET SCIENCE

Rewire Your Thinking

BETH BIANCA

Blue PLUTO Publishing

"MINDSET SCIENCE: *Rewire Your Thinking*"

MINDSET SCIENCE: *Rewire Your Thinking* / Beth Bianca --1st ed.

ISBN-13: 978-0-578-43203-8

Join Beth Bianca's motivational community, using your phone.
Text LIVING to 444999.

Learn more at www.BethBianca.com

DISCLAIMER: This publication, and the information presented herein, is provided for informational and educational purposes only and is not to be interpreted as an endorsement of a particular plan, product, or course of action. Beth Bianca and Blue Pluto Publishing are not medical or health care providers, and the information presented in this publication is not intended as medical or professional advice, nor as a substitute for or alternative to medical treatment. You should consult with a qualified professional before beginning this or any other exercise or nutrition program. In addition, health and fitness information and research changes rapidly and varies from person to person, and some information presented herein may be out of date or may not apply to your specific circumstances. Use of this publication and the information presented herein, especially prior to consulting a qualified professional, is at your sole choice and risk. The author and publisher specifically disclaim any responsibility for any liability, loss, or risk, personal or otherwise, which is incurred as a consequence, directly or indirectly, of the use and application of any of the contents of this book.

Edited by Lydia Lazar

DEDICATION

Dedicated to my Mom, Lou Lou, who was the warmest, most loving person I've ever known. I was blessed beyond words to be your daughter.

ACKNOWLEDGMENTS

I thank God every day for this second opportunity at life.

Thank you to my friend and editor Lydia Lazar. Without your help, this book would not have been possible. Your ideas, encouragement, and support gave me the confidence to put these words out into the world.

Thank you to all my "peeps" including my aunt Nancy, sister Carlene, niece Bella, and dear friends Gina and Robin. Your encouragement, support and friendship make my world brighter.

ALSO BY BETH BIANCA

Mindset Breakthrough: *Achieve Weight-Loss Surgery Success*

The Breakthrough Journal: *Butterfly Edition*

The Breakthrough Journal: *Flower Edition*

Mindset Reminder: *365 Days of Inspiring Quotes and Contemplations to Discover Your Inner Strength and Transform Your Life from the Inside Out*

Use the following link to download PDF versions of all the worksheets included in this book: https://BigBrightWhy.com/worksheets/

TABLE OF CONTENTS

INTRODUCTION

Does life seem like a constant struggle of ups and downs? Are you frustrated because, every time you try to change a behavior, you just end up back where you started? Do you want to stop the roller coaster ride and get off?

There is hope. Neuroscience researchers have been studying why certain people can change their negative behaviors, while others continue to struggle. They have been publishing their research for years. And yet, the self-help industry keeps selling their same old advice, which only gives us pieces of a bigger puzzle.

I banged my head against a wall for years while reading books, going to seminars, and buying audio sessions. I was desperately searching for an escape route to set me free. But nothing ever worked, and I always went back to the same self-defeating behaviors.

My roller coaster ride didn't stop—it crashed.

You will read more about that in Chapter Three, but the short story is that I ended up weighing 394 pounds, lost my health, lost my livelihood, and was in a state of pure survival. Even after having weight loss surgery to save my life, the self-defeating behaviors were still embedded in my brain. I had two choices: find a way to change the behaviors or prepare for the grimmest of consequences.

Slowly, I uncovered more pieces of the bigger puzzle. Some came from books while others seemed to happen by chance. And then one day, my behaviors began to shift. I had finally found the cryptic escape route. My self-defeating habits no longer held me captive.

It was true freedom.

I lost 224 pounds, have maintained my weight loss, and achieved my childhood dream of becoming a published author. Not too bad after thirty years of trying.

How did these positive behaviors transform into my "new normal" way of being? That is the reason for this book.

Inside these pages, you will learn the neuroscience research of how our brains work, and why the brain keeps us stuck in current behavior patterns. And then, you'll discover your own escape route. Imagine living the life you want, without the struggle of guilt, frustration, and self-sabotage.

You can stop the roller coaster and step off. Don't wait until it crashes like I did. Choose to be in control.

Let's get started!

CHAPTER ONE

YOUR PAST DOESN'T PREDICT YOUR FUTURE

Your past is just a story. And once you realize this, it has no power over you. ~Chuck Palahniuk

You are destined for greatness!

What was your first thought after reading that sentence? Did you think, *yay, I've got this*? Or, did you think, *yeah, right, you have no idea what I've been through during my life*? No matter what your first thought was, you are right. The way you think creates the reality you see in your world.

Life is like a mirror that reflects what we believe back for us to see. When you stand in front of a mirror, you see a reflection of yourself. Have you ever stepped in front of the mirror and expected to see someone else's reflection? Of course not. So, why would we think our views about life have nothing to do with the life we experience?

Now imagine that, while looking in the mirror, you noticed your hair wasn't quite right. Would you try fixing the reflection? No, you would fix the hair on your head and then look to see the results reflected in the mirror. That is how making changes in our lives work as well.

When we notice something requires a change, we need to correct the cause of the problem, which is our thinking. Only then will we see the changes reflected in our life experiences. Remember, we didn't work with the mirror to change the reflection of messed hair; we corrected the actual problem, which was the hair itself.

If you constantly think about the failures of your past, how can your reality be any different today? You cannot achieve any more than you believe is possible. But the good news is, you do not have to stay stuck in the struggle. You can change your thinking and your future. We now have research to prove that changes are possible at any point during life.

The reason we can change is summed up with one word: **Neuroplasticity**.

Neuroplasticity is a big word with a very hopeful meaning. It's the brain's ability to change and adapt throughout our lifetime. Everything we think and do is either re-enforcing a neural pathway or creating a new one.

The mental health agency West Texas Centers [Ref-1] clarifies the concept like this: "Very simply, neuroplasticity is all about neurons having the ability to establish new connections throughout our brains, facilitating all sorts of fresh functioning. So, it's about a rewiring of the brain."

The BrainWorksNeurotherapy.com [Ref-2] website describes neuroplasticity this way: "With every repetition of a thought or emotion, we reinforce a neural pathway - and with each new thought, we begin to create a new way of being. These small changes, frequently enough repeated, lead to changes in how our brains work."

What this means is that we are not doomed to stay the same. Our past mistakes do not have to dictate our future outcomes. There really is hope because we can change! That is pretty exciting stuff.

What's important for you to understand is that your past is over. We have no control over what was or who we have been. But, we do have control over who we decide to become.

Now you have a choice: you can continue living the way you have been or you can create a brand-new tomorrow.

I'm guessing, since you're reading this book, you are ready to create a new tomorrow. Let's get to work!

Look back only for as long as you must,
Then go forward into the history you will make.
Alberto Rios
from "A House Called Tomorrow"

MINDSET SCIENCE

CHAPTER TWO

THIS TIME IS DIFFERENT

You are creating, at this moment, the person you're going to become tomorrow, and you are physically wiring that person into your brain.
~Shad Helmstetter, Ph.D.

This time is going to be different because it's not like all the other times you tried to make a change and ended up right back where you started. If you apply what you learn in these pages, you will see the results that have eluded you for years.

I'm going to explain how you can rewire your brain in simple and understandable terms. I love using analogies to make a point because they are easier to understand. So, get ready for all sorts of analogies ahead. You have been forewarned.

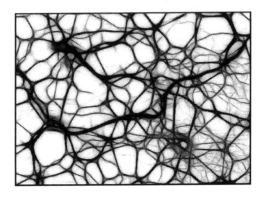

(i-1) Image of neural pathways in the brain.

Follow along with me while looking at the image (i-1). It's labeled as being neural pathways in the brain; however, I would like you to picture a roadmap. Some of the lines are thicker and darker, while others are smaller and fainter in the background. The darker lines represent major highways, and the fainter lines represent small local roads.

Obviously, the major highways are where you travel the most. These are the thoughts and behaviors that you consistently repeat. They are very easy to use and have become second nature to you. Most of the time you don't even consciously think about them. They are your habits.

The small local roads are the thoughts and actions you don't use often. They are small and faint because of the low amount of traffic. These roads are not as easy to use; there are holes, detours, and narrow lanes. You have to consciously think about using these small roads because it doesn't come naturally for you. They represent the times you tried using willpower to make changes in your life, but ended up going back to the major highway instead.

For example, let's use someone who loves sitting on the couch and watching TV every night. Then, one day they decide they want to start exercising. Their current high-speed highway is sitting on the couch every night. Their new slow backroad is starting to exercise. In the beginning, it is much easier to stay on the major highway rather than taking the slow backroad. Many people refer to making this kind of change as the "struggle."

A lot of the time, our past missteps have to do with how these highways and roads were wired into our brain. These paths were usually formed without us even being aware of them.

Our current pathways were created by our experiences, beliefs, dominant thoughts, what we read, what we watch, what we listen to, and the people around us. Our brains record every moment of every day and use that information to map out our pathways.

You know those times when you feel like you are fighting yourself? The times when you are sabotaging all your hard efforts? That is because your subconscious mind keeps taking you back to the easy major highways.

An article in PsychologyToday.com [Ref-3] by Rebecca Gladding, M.D., co-author of *You Are Not Your Brain*, explains, " . . . many of the thoughts, impulses, urges and sensations we experience do not reflect who we are or the life we want to live. These false missives are not true representations of us, but rather are inaccurate, and highly deceptive, brain messages."

This research shows that our past missteps were caused by wiring we were not even aware of having.

When I read the following quote, it really hit home. Those of us who have tried to accomplish something over and over again can definitely relate.

> "In short, the brain likely has run your life in a less than optimal way and caused you to experience one or more of the following at some point in your life: anxiety, self-doubt, perfectionism, behaving in ways or engaging in habits that are not good for you . . . ignoring your true self and/or wholeheartedly believing the stream of negative thoughts coursing through your head." PsychologyToday.com [Ref-4].

So now you have an idea of how your brain has been influencing your behavior. The chapters ahead will show how to consciously create your new high-speed highways, your new ways of thinking and experiencing the world. You can become the person you CHOOSE TO BE instead of just settling for the way things have always been.

Two roads diverged in a wood, and I —
I took the one less travelled by,
And that has made all the difference.

Robert Frost
from "The Road Not Taken"

MINDSET SCIENCE

CHAPTER THREE

IT WAS ALL IN MY MIND

Sometimes to self-discover you must self-destruct. ~Robert M. Drake

For those of you who tend to believe you can never change, there is hope. But the hope is contingent on you believing that change is possible.

It's a bit of a conundrum, isn't it? If you were already a positive thinker, your brain would be wired differently. That's not to say that people who are optimistic have a brain that's perfectly wired.

As I look back on my life, there were periods where I was optimistic. But, there were also times where I was clinically depressed. There always seemed to be a trigger that would initiate the change in my thinking. And once those thoughts began, it was like falling into a hole that I couldn't escape.

My last bout of depression began around the start of the Great Recession in 2008 and lasted for seven years. During that time, I decided to give up on trying to lose weight because I was convinced I'd never win that battle. And so began the downward spiral to one of the lowest points of my life.

At first, there was a sense of freedom. I could eat whatever I wanted, in any portion size I wanted.

Gone was the guilt, the nagging voice in my head saying *I shouldn't eat that* or *I should do this instead*. I was like a kid in the candy store.

While enjoying my new food freedom, I was working on strategies for my small business. As the economy had become worse, I was implementing changes that would allow us to weather the storm. I just didn't realize how big and long the storm was going to be.

By 2011 I went from weighing 260 pounds up to 340 pounds. Yes, my food freedom was working really well. I had proved that I was never going to be thin. I'd grown out of multiple clothing sizes and started having problems breathing.

My business wasn't doing so well, either. One by one, my clients were being laid off from their jobs and no longer needed our services. We had put up a gallant fight, but the economy just wasn't getting any better. Now that my health had begun to deteriorate, I couldn't fight for my breath and the business at the same time. I had to let my business go.

I used to think, "If I'm never going to be thin, at least I can be a successful businesswoman." But that was no longer the case. After nine years, my sense of pride from building a business from scratch into a profitable revenue generator had come to an end. I felt lost.

When 2013 came rolling around, things weren't getting any better. I tried to find a job, but my current health condition prevented it. I couldn't walk more than a few steps without being out of breath. I had stopped weighing myself because I was afraid to know what the scale would show. I avoided mirrors. I didn't recognize the person I had become.

By September, I couldn't hide my condition any further. It was obvious to everyone around me that something was wrong. Either I had become extremely lazy, or I was seriously sick.

Funny as it sounds now, I didn't want to see a doctor because I knew they would weigh me. And after that, they would say I had to lose weight. Yeah, right. Me lose weight? We all knew that wasn't going to happen.

To appease my sister and best friend, I finally went to the doctor. To my surprise, losing weight wasn't the first thing I heard. My doctor listened to all my symptoms and ordered a whole bunch of tests. After a few visits, I was ready to hear what was happening. Had I just become a big, lazy baby and was making a mountain out of a molehill, or was there something more going on?

The good news: I was not a big, lazy baby. The bad news: I was diagnosed with pulmonary hypertension. That was the reason I couldn't take more than a couple of steps without being out of breath. Some of the arteries in my lungs were damaged, and blood could not flow through the way it should.

As if having pulmonary hypertension wasn't enough, I also had both obstructive and central sleep apnea as well as high blood pressure, type 2 diabetes, a fatty liver, and three herniated discs in my back. And after that, I heard the words I had expected, "Losing weight would help improve all these issues."

Losing weight might not *cure* all my ailments, but it would definitely help. I was in a serious predicament. Those last couple months of 2013 were very dark days.

As 2014 rolled in, I was using a bi-pap machine, which worked like a ventilator, to help me breath at night; and I was on multiple medications. Yet, my health was still getting worse.

My doctor brought up having weight-loss surgery. It was our last opportunity to help my worsening condition. It took months to get to the first surgery consultation, and I remember it vividly. When I stepped on the scale, I weighed 394 pounds.

Seven months passed between the first surgery consultation and the day of my surgery. During that time, my condition continued to deteriorate. I was confined to a wheelchair and only left my home for doctor visits. I lived alone, so my sister had to come over to take my fur-baby for walks and help take care of me. I was merely existing and just waiting to die. I started making my funeral plans to make things easier for everyone after the inevitable happened.

I'm sharing this with you because I want you to see how far gone my thoughts were. Before my breakthrough, I was negative, felt dark inside, and had a bleak future. I had rewired my brain to create the worst circumstances possible. But at that time, I didn't realize that was happening. I don't think any of us knows when we're doing that to ourselves.

By my surgery day, I was a high-risk patient. But even my surgeon said there wasn't much of a choice left for me. The upside was that, if everything worked out okay, I would have a chance of saving my life.

As you probably already guessed, I made it through the surgery. Yay!!

My recovery took longer than most; and even after losing over 100 pounds, I was still not able to walk without being out of breath. But, my condition stopped getting worse.

One thing that hadn't changed yet was my negative thinking. I kept wondering if the pulmonary hypertension symptoms would ever improve or if I would be confined to a wheelchair for the rest of my life.

Although I had been losing weight, my mind was still craving the food I loved and missed. I was torturing myself. I just wanted to eat like normal—my normal.

What can I do to make this situation better?

That was actually the first positive thought I had in seven years. I pulled out old motivational books and started to read them again. I opened the door to thinking maybe my life wasn't over.

Maybe there was a future, and maybe I could have dreams and goals again.

The process of rewiring my brain didn't happen overnight. It took time and effort to switch out all the negative thinking I had built over seven years. But I did change the wiring and began the journey of becoming who I am today.

It took two years, one month, and one day from my first surgery consultation until the day I reached my goal weight. I lost a total of 224 pounds, regained my life, and began pursuing the dreams I had always kept on the back burner.

And I'm not finished. God gave me a second chance to live, and I'm not going to mess it up this time.

There is hope for everyone. I want to yell from the rooftops:

OUR PAST DOESN'T PREDICT OUR FUTURE!!

This book is part of the vision I developed for my life in the summer of 2015. I wish I had known about neuroplasticity sooner. But it was all part of my journey. Now, your journey can be easier. If you so choose.

How first I entered on that path astray,
Beset with sleep, I know not.

Dante Alighieri
from "Inferno"

MINDSET SCIENCE

CHAPTER FOUR

A WONDERFUL DISCOVERY

Every man can, if he so desires, become the sculptor of his own brain." ~Santiago Ramon y Cajal

Technological advances have helped neuroscientists to see the inner workings of the brain. As science goes, neuroplasticity is a rather new discovery. But it is providing hope for people looking to make changes in their lives, as well as those suffering from brain disorders and injuries.

Before neuroplasticity, neuroscientists believed the adult brain was fixed. In other words, we were stuck with the cards dealt to us. That included, among other things, our IQs and happiness thresholds. How sad is that? No pun intended. For us regular folks, it is a good thing most of us didn't know that. We were supposed to be stuck our entire adult life. Who wants to think they can never rise above a certain level of happiness or can't improve our intelligence by learning something new? That certainly paints a bleak picture.

Although research now shows our brains can be rewired, too many people still live with a fixed mindset. They either don't know of the possibility to change or simply choose not to believe it's possible for them.

Step One of rewiring your brain is for you to open the door to believing change is possible for yourself. Believing change is NOT possible for yourself definitely makes it impossible.

Remember, I started my journey out of depression with a single thought. You can do the same. Open the door right now by telling yourself *change is possible for me*. Then repeat that to yourself all day long. And keep repeating it every day until you feel excitement building inside your gut. That is all it takes to start; just be open.

Here is more evidence of how amazing our brain is. Professor of Neurology at Harvard Medical School Alvaro Pascual-Leone, M.D., Ph.D. [Ref-5] conducted a study where the participants were instructed to play the piano for two hours every day for five days. At the end of each practice, they were hooked up for a brain test that mapped out the neurons used for their piano-playing finger movements.

At the end of the study, Dr. Pascual-Leon found that the participants' neurons increased and took over the surrounding areas of the brain. And that was just after five days! The findings showed that the more we use a particular area of the brain, the more that area of the brain grows. The brain actually creates more space for the neurons we use the most. Sound familiar? Those are the major highways from our brain map in Chapter One.

Our brains get better at doing whatever we give them to do. And that is not just for positive functions. If you consistently give your brain things to worry about, your brain will get really good at worrying. You will end up having more neurons devoted to worrying. That's not the kind of wiring we want to create or re-enforce.

Even before I knew of this study, I often wrote about the concept that *what we focus on grows* in our lives. Our thoughts are more powerful than we realize. Look at your life and see where your thoughts have brought you. It is all there in the roadmap of your wiring.

Let's get back to Dr. Pascual-Leon and his revealing studies. After completing the piano-playing/neuron study, he took it a step further. He instructed another group of piano players to practice the piano for two hours, five days in a row, but to only think about playing the piano while keeping their hands still. They were to imagine the finger movements of playing the piano in their heads.

At the end of the second study, the results showed the same neuron growth as the first group. The second group's neurons grew from imagining they were playing the piano, while the first group actually played it. That is absolutely amazing! Just thinking can spark neurons!

Dr. Pascual-Leon's findings prove that our thoughts do have the power to rewire our brain. His study also shows that visualization has the same effects on the brain as does an actual experience.

You can read more about this study in the Time Magazine article [Ref-5], The Brain: How the Brain Rewires Itself.

We will be learning more about visualization in the coming chapters. Right now, remember Step

One is to open the door to believing change is possible for you.

What is now proved was once, only imagin'd.

~William Blake
from "The Marriage of Heaven and Hell"

MINDSET SCIENCE

CHAPTER FIVE

YOUR BIG BRIGHT WHY

If you want to be happy, set a goal that commands your thoughts, liberates your energy and inspires your hopes. ~Andrew Carnegie

Our brain knows how to wire itself. That is pretty obvious because we've all had wiring installed without our conscious input. The real work starts when we decide to change that wiring.

Rewiring our brain to stay on a newly created path is going to take time and effort. The brain's natural tendency is to lead us back to a well-travelled high-speed highway.

Remember the piano-playing study in Chapter Four? The participant's neurons grew within five days. But they practiced for two hours every day. And both groups already knew how to play the piano. Dr. Pascual-Leon's study helped them re-enforce a road that was already mapped in their brain and turn it into a high-speed highway.

For us, this means we can re-enforce an existing road faster than creating a brand-new path from nothing. So depending on the goal we choose, the time involved will vary. But effort is definitely required for any changes we decide to make.

Those who are committed to doing the work will see positive results. Those who are not committed and become easily distracted will most likely not have lasting changes. And some people will end up re-enforcing an existing high-speed highway instead of creating the new path they desired.

The secret to being committed enough to do the hard work is by having a big enough "why" for creating the new path.

What follows is a very unscientific term to describe this, but it's accurate:

Wishy-washy goals lead to wishy-washy results.

It's that simple.

Step Two of rewiring your brain is for you to find your Big Bright Why.

Your Big Bright Why will keep you focused on your goal for the entire time it takes to achieve it. Think about how people make New Year's resolutions. Those first couple of weeks, everyone is so motivated. They are determined to make the new year ahead better than all the others before. And then, by the middle of February, most people have given up and have gone right back to their normal routines. Or, I should say, to their high-speed highways.

The same thing happens when you set a new goal. People usually set a goal to do something they have never done before. In the beginning, they are motivated to make changes and are focused on seeing their results. But if their reason for wanting the goal is not strong enough, they will give up easily when a challenge or obstacle appears.

Elliot Berkman, an Associate Professor in the Department of Psychology at the University of Oregon [Ref-6], explains the issue with goals as this: "Goals are usually things we want but have difficulty achieving even when we know they are achievable."

That's what happened to me every time I started a diet. It would go well for a period of time; but, eventually, I went right back to my high-speed highway of negative habits. Sometimes it felt like I was diligently looking for something to take me off course so I could go back to my old ways.

Trying to make changes by using willpower alone works for a little while. But, eventually, the willpower seems to fade and so do the behavior changes we were working to develop. We need to rewire our brain to make permanent changes in our behavior.

Having a Big Bright Why not only gives us the motivation to start creating a new path, it keeps us motivated to continue using that path until it becomes a new high-speed highway.

Now you know the importance of having a "why." It's time for you to discover yours. A Big Bright Why is deeply personal and tied to the values you hold near and dear.

In volume five of the Neuro Leadership Journal [Ref-7], titled *AIM: An Integrative Model of Goal Pursuit*, the authors write, "We are motivated by the "why" of goals and their broader implications. . .."

Here's an example: Jennifer wants to start her own business. By itself, that is a goal; but it's not a Big Bright Why. The "broader implications" referred to in the previous quote are Jennifer's reward for having her own business. Having a business is a nice thought, but it is not motivating enough to overcome the challenges which will inevitably occur. What is more motivating is all the positive ways Jennifer's life will change as a result of having her own business.

Jennifer will get a better idea of what her Big Bright Why is by using the following **Q**uestion and **A**nswer strategy.

Q: Why do I want to start my own business?

A: *I'm tired of working for a big corporation.*

Q: Why am I tired of working for a big corporation?

A: *Because of the bureaucracy and uncertainty.*

Q: What bothers me about the bureaucracy and uncertainty?

A: *Nothing gets accomplished because management is afraid to change the status quo. And I never know when the next downsizing is going to happen. There's no job security.*

Q: Why do I think that having my own business will alleviate those problems?

A: *I know starting my own business won't be easy. But I'll be responsible for the decisions that affect my income instead of being dependent on the decisions made by upper managers. And I won't be waiting for another round of layoffs, wondering if I'm on the list. I just crave freedom. And I want to make a difference in people's lives instead of helping a big corporation get richer.*

See how Jennifer found the real reasons for wanting to start her business? Having freedom and helping people are values that are important to her. Now she's closer to discovering her Big Bright Why.

Knowing the deeper meaning behind her goal will help Jennifer to develop a picture of what her life will look like when she has her own business.

Here is Jennifer's list of positive changes that will happen when she has her business.

- I'll be free from the corporate world! I'll spend my days building a business that makes me proud. My decisions, my results, my future.
- I'll be doing something I love while helping people, too.
- My schedule will be flexible, so I can be available for family when they need me.
- I'll work from wherever I want to work. No more stuffy office.

We can see the importance of Jennifer's feelings of freedom coming through when she describes how her life will be when she achieves her goal.

Here is Jennifer's Big Bright Why Statement: *My Big Bright Why is to create a business that allows me the freedom of living life on my terms. A business where I can help people improve their lives—a business that rewards me for the effort I put forth.*

Hopefully, you can see from this example how much more exciting and motivating a Big Bright Why is, compared to a generic goal like saying *I want to start a business.*

The Neuro Leadership Journal [Ref-7] article continues, "A feeling of achievement (Status) competence, (Autonomy), or belongingness (Relatedness) all activate the primary reward network of the brain, which means they impart an intensely rewarding experience."

Activating those feelings will keep your motivation high enough to withstand the challenges and obstacles that will inevitably show up on the way to achieving your goal. You will be harnessing a force much stronger than using willpower alone.

Something to remember is that your "why" is about what you want, not what someone else thinks is important for you. Studies have shown that being motivated by an outside source is not enough to keep people from quitting when they come up against challenges.

PNAS.org [Ref-8] published a study from Yale University. During a span of fourteen years, they evaluated West Point Cadets. They found the cadets who entered the academy because of deeply desired internal motives achieved more during the fourteen-year study than those who entered the academy due to outside motivation, such as influence from family and friends.

When discovering your Big Bright Why, you will have to put your inner critic away. Do not start this process with any judgment in your mind. Allow your thoughts to flow freely. Whatever crosses your mind, write down without hesitation.

Use the example of Jennifer's questions and answers to begin the process. There also is a worksheet at the end of this chapter. If you have no idea where to start, here are some suggestions to help you think through the process of discovering your Big Bright Why.

- Write out a list of 100 things you would like to do during your lifetime. The first twenty should be easy to do; but, after that, you'll need to give it more thought. The deeper you dig, the more surprised you will be by what you discover. An article in Harvard Business Review [Ref-9] cited an experiment at Northwestern University by psychologists Brian Lucas and Loran Nordgren. They found the first 20 ideas people generated were "conventional." After the initial 20 ideas, the participants found "more-unusual possibilities."

- What were your childhood dreams?
- What would you do if you knew you couldn't fail?
- What is important to you and why?
- What are your passions?
- What brings you the greatest joy?
- How does your ideal life look?

Here's a clue to know when you've discovered your Big Bright Why: you'll get a great big smile on your face whenever you think about it. If there's no smile, that's not your "why."

An article in Mental Health Daily [Ref-10] titled "Self-Directed Neuroplasticity: Consciously Changing Your Brain Function" describes the importance of motivation in changing neural pathways this way, "The more you really want to change, the more effort you are going to make in order to get over the hump. Passion is what separates the people who get results and change from the people who stagnate in the same neural "ruts."

Remember, your Big Bright Why will be your driving force. It's the spark that ignites the flame that fuels the motivation to keep moving toward your goal.

Have fun discovering your Big Bright Why. Besides getting crystal clear on what you want, it's also pretty darn therapeutic too.

Now it's time to learn how we begin creating those new paths.

And then the day came,
when the risk
to remain tight
in a bud
was more painful
than the risk
it took
to blossom.

Anais Nin
the poem "Risk"

BIG BRIGHT WHY WORKSHEET

What is your starting goal?
Why do you want to do this?
Why is that?
Why is that important?
Is that reason strong enough to keep you focused and determined to push through challenges?
If "**no**," keep asking "why" questions. If you still can't answer "yes," a different starting goal may need consideration. Review Chapter Five again.
If your answer was "**yes**," List all the positive changes that will happen when you reach this goal on the next worksheet.

BIG BRIGHT WHY WORKSHEET

List all the positive changes that will happen when you reach your Big Bright Why. How will your life be different?

Create your Big Bright Why statement.

Does that statement make you feel excited?
If not, keep working on the statement until it does.

MINDSET SCIENCE

CHAPTER SIX

WE BECOME WHAT WE REPEATEDLY DO

As a single footstep will not make a path on the earth, so a single thought will not make a pathway in the mind. ~Henry David Thoreau

While researching this book, I read that people do not like to be called "creatures of habit." I'd never thought about that being an issue because a large part of our daily activities are completed without any conscious thought. An article in ScienceDaily.com [Ref-11] states, "About 40 percent of people's daily activities are performed each day in almost the same situations."

The subject of habits brings us right back to the image [i-1] in Chapter Two, our brain's high-speed highways. Almost half our daily activities are driven by cues in our environment instead of by our conscious thought.

Our amazing brains like to make things easier for us. Once an action is repeated consistently enough within the same environment, a habit is formed. Once that action becomes a habit, the brain moves that activity to another area where it no longer requires our conscious thought.

A simple example of this is locking the door when you are leaving home. You could be halfway to your destination and ask yourself, *did I lock the door?* That is because you have no conscious memory of locking the door when you left.

The brain uses the cues in our environment to activate the appropriate action when it is needed. In our example; walking out of your home cued the action of locking the door. All this leaves more neuron space available for the actions that require our conscious thoughts to perform.

Since most of our habits were created without us really knowing it, we have used this amazing ability to create habits that are now in conflict with our new goals. That is why knowing your Big Bright Why is so important to rewiring your neurons.

> "Longtime habits are literally entrenched at the neural level, so they are powerful determinants of behavior. The good news is that

people are nearly always capable of doing something else when they're made aware of the habit and are sufficiently motivated to change." HopesandFears.com [Ref-12], Neuroscientist Elliot Berman, Ph.D.

Step Three of rewiring your brain is for you to choose a negative habit that you want to reroute.

- Take a sheet of paper or use the worksheet at the end of this chapter and write down the habits that are your current high-speed highways. Some of your behaviors will be easy to pinpoint. But, also think about your automatic behaviors, the things you do without thinking about them. You may have to monitor yourself for a day or two to become aware of all the things you do unconsciously.

- Next to each high-speed highway habit, answer the following question: is this behavior bringing me closer to my goal or further from it?

- On a scale from one to ten, mark each behavior that is taking you further from your goal, with one not being very far and ten being the farthest away from your goal.

- Choose the high-speed highway that is a number ten or closest to a ten as your first habit marked for rerouting.

You will most likely discover more than one habit that will need to be rerouted. Just pick one to get started. After you have made progress on the first habit, you can begin working on the next one. The important thing right now is to make this process easy for yourself. Trying to do too much at once will derail your chances of making any progress. You don't want to quit before you've even started.

There is a saying I've read many times: "A confused mind always says no." Remember this as we work through this process. It really fits with what we are doing.

Back to the article in HopeandFears.com [Ref-12], Elliot Berkman, Ph.D. explains, "It's much easier to start doing something new than to stop doing something habitual without a replacement behavior."

Step Four of rewiring your brain is for you to choose a positive habit to replace the negative habit you chose at Step Three.

Grab another sheet of paper or use the worksheet at the end of this chapter and write down your main goal—the big goal that led you to find your Big Bright Why. Now we are going to break that goal down into smaller action-oriented goals. These Action Goals will become the behaviors that form your new high-speed highways.

Action Goals are behaviors you have control over. They cannot depend on someone else helping you or rely on results outside of your control. Saying you want to lose three pounds in a week is not an Action Goal. You can not control the amount of weight you lose in a week. The scale doesn't always reflect the changes in your body. What you can control are the actions you take to lose three pounds. For instance, you have control over when you exercise and how many calories you eat in a day. The same holds true for getting a promotion at work. You cannot control the decisions of upper management, but you can control the actions that make you a candidate for a promotion. A strong action goal is to show up to work on time and perform your responsibilities in a quick and efficient manner. When you stick with behaviors you control, you'll be setting yourself up for a win instead of a disappointment.

In an article in Psychology Today [Ref-13], author Ralph Ryback, M.D. explains, "The satisfaction of ticking off a small task is linked with a flood of dopamine. Each time your brain gets a whiff of this rewarding neurotransmitter, it will want you to repeat the associated behavior."

There is more than one purpose for having Action Goals.

- They break a large goal down into manageable pieces.

- They give you small wins that help build your confidence.
- They give you the "how" for reaching your Big Bright Why.

In volume five of the Neuro Leadership Journal [Ref-7] titled *AIM: An Integrative Model of Goal Pursuit*, the authors write, "Success at a goal requires both a will and a way, both the why and the how."

Let's use Jennifer as an example again. She may not yet know all the steps involved with reaching her goal, but she can start with what she knows right now.

The important part is to get started instead of waiting for the perfect time. There is never a perfect time. Or, I should say, right now is the perfect time to get started.

Q: What can I do right now that will bring me closer to starting my business?

- I can start saving money for the start-up, plus enough to cover my personal expenses for at least a year.
- I can start networking with other professionals and business owners
- I can take a course on creating a business plan.

Now we can create Jennifer's first Action Goal.

I will save at least $300 per week.

We will be using the **S.M.A.R.T**. acronym to make sure it is a good action-oriented goal.

- **Specific:** *Yes, save at least $300.*
- **Measurable**: *Yes, $300.*
- **Actionable:** *Yes, she will personally save.*

- **Realistic:** *Yes, at her current income level.*

- **Time Bound:** *Yes, every week.*

Let's create a second Action Goal for Jennifer.

I will attend two networking events every month.

- **Specific**: *Yes, attend two networking events.*

- **Measurable**: *Yes, two events.*

- **Actionable**: *Yes, she will be going to the meetings.*

- **Realistic**: *Yes, it is very doable.*

- **Time Bound**: *Yes, every month.*

Here are examples of what are not good Action Goals.

- I will try to save some money.

- I will go to networking events.

You can see the difference between the SMART Action Goals and the wishy-washy goals. Jennifer will definitely know if she has accomplished her savings goal every week and her networking goal every month.

Now Jennifer knows exactly what to do this week to get closer to her Big Bright Why. And she will begin creating new neural paths for her high-speed highways.

Remember the adage "A confused mind always says no." Keeping your first week simple is the key to making this work. You want to start with a win, and you do that by not making it too difficult.

After a successful week, you can add something new to conquer. But you need to give yourself a "win" before moving on to the next stage. We are looking to create long-term, sustainable results, not another crash-and-burn scenario.

Now, you have chosen a habit to reroute, picked a new behavior to implement, and learned how to set up your Action Goals. In the next chapter, we'll start the rerouting sequence.

Not enjoyment, and not sorrow,
Is our destined end or way;
But to act, that each tomorrow
Find us farther than today.

Henry Wadsworth Longfellow
from "Voices of the Night"

NEGATIVE HABIT WORKSHEET

Column 1	2	3

- **Column 1**: Write out the behaviors that are your current high-speed highways.
- **Column 2**: Is this behavior bringing you closer to your Big Bright Why? Yes or No
- **Column 3**: On a scale from 1-10, mark each behavior that is taking you further from your Big Bright Why, with one not being too far and ten being the farthest away.

Choose the habit that's a number ten or closest to a ten as your first behavior to reroute. Write it below.

ACTION GOALS WORKSHEET

Starting Goal:
What can I do right now to bring me closer to my Big Bright Why Goal?   1.   2.   3.   Convert these answers into S.M.A.R.T. Action Goals.
Action Goal: Specific: Measurable: Actionable: Realistic: Time Bound:
Action Goal: Specific: Measurable: Actionable: Realistic: Time Bound:
Action Goal: Specific: Measurable: Actionable: Realistic: Time Bound:

CHAPTER SEVEN

DETOUR AHEAD

All things are difficult before they become easy.
~Saadi

Remember how it felt riding a bicycle for the first time. It wasn't easy, was it? But over time, riding your bike every day became second nature to you. You no longer had to concentrate on balancing yourself. You just hopped on your bike and took off! Even after not riding a bike for years, you can still ride easily.

It was the same way with learning how to drive. I remember the first time I sat behind the wheel and had to think about everything I was doing. How much pressure should I put on the gas pedal? Don't push the brake too fast. Which way does the turn signal work? But over time, driving became as automatic as riding a bike. There were times I drove from my home to work and didn't even remember the drive at all.

Those are two perfect examples of how our brain wiring works. At first, everything takes time to learn and apply. We have to put in the effort to build those paths. But over time it becomes easier because our brain has sent that activity to the automatic "cue and response" center of our brain. Now those actions are part of our high-speed highways.

Putting in the effort to wire those highways didn't seem like work. We couldn't wait to ride a bike or gain our freedom by being able to drive.

Knowing your Big Bright Why should make the effort of rewiring your brain just as exciting now. If you are not that excited about making the changes ahead, you may want to revisit Chapter Five.

Let's begin setting up a big detour sign over the habit you have already chosen to reroute. An article at SPSP.org [Ref-14] states, "Work from Verplanken and colleagues show [sic] habits can be changed when you change the factors around the habit (location, context). Researchers call this the "discontinuity effect."

Simply stated, the "discontinuity effect" means changing the routine you have developed around that behavior/habit.

For instance, I always ate in front of the television. When I began to change my thoughts about food, I read about mindful eating. What I had been doing was the epitome of *mindless* eating. My mind was busy watching TV instead of concentrating on my meal. The result was never being satisfied after a meal. I'd start planning what snack I would eat next.

Without knowing anything about the discontinuity effect, I decided to not eat in front of the TV. I began eating every meal without watching or reading anything. My mind was now able to focus on the food I was eating, and that resulted in being more satisfied with my new healthy meals. Within a couple of weeks, my cravings for the food I used to eat in front of the TV were gone.

I broke that cue and changed my routine. That allowed me to begin the process of rewiring my brain about eating healthy food. I no longer felt deprived about missing the high fat, high-calorie foods I had eaten my whole life.

When I saw the results of making that change, I began changing other routines as well. Every time I changed a routine, I changed a negative habit. I wondered why I had not realized that sooner.

Step Five of rewiring your brain is for you to identify the cue that initiates the bad-habit routine, and then disrupt it. There is a worksheet to use at the end of this chapter.

Remember what we learned in Chapter Six. Every habit has a cue which triggers the behavior. That is how our brain works. Start to monitor your daily routines to find the cue that sparks your unwanted behavior. When you discover the cue, develop a plan to disrupt it, effectively shutting down that routine.

The article in ScienceDaily.com [Ref-11] states, "First, you must derail existing habits and create a window of opportunity to act on new intentions. . . When the cues for existing habits are removed, it's easier to form a new behavior."

The article continues to say a great time to disrupt habits is when people move or change jobs. I think that's great if you're planning to make those changes. But for a lot of us, that really isn't an option. Try doing something easier, like I did with not eating while watching TV. Or, if you have trouble getting up in the morning, change the sound of your alarm. Then use the new alarm cue to trigger the new behavior of getting out of bed, instead of hitting the snooze button.

Once you find the cues/triggers, remove them from your environment. Do anything that makes it more difficult to act on that behavior. If there are cues in an area that you don't have control over, visualize a big DETOUR sign whenever or wherever that cue occurs. Then develop a plan to remove yourself from that area.

The article in Psychology Today [Ref-13] states, "Environmental cues are essential when it comes to habit formation, in part because the brain is excellent at connecting an environment with a specific situation."

Disrupting the current cues is necessary for rewiring your brain. Just remember, everything is hard at first, then it becomes easier. Look for ways to make these changes work instead of reasons why they won't.

Another way to reroute your current high-speed highways is by disrupting the reward you perceive from that behavior.

Step Six of rewiring your brain is for you to identify the reward you receive from the habit you chose to reroute and then disrupt it.

In the HopeandFears.com article [Ref-12], Susan Krauss Whitbourne, Ph.D. explains, "Breaking a habit means that you break the link between the behavior and the reward it provides to you."

Using the example of not getting up when your alarm goes off, the current reward is going back to sleep. When the new alarm sounds, instead of staying comfortable under your covers, make it harder for yourself to fall back asleep. That could be as simple as having a bright light go on above your head. The key is to break the link between the behavior of not getting up and the reward of going back to sleep.

I inadvertently applied this approach years ago when I ate too many onion rings before getting the stomach flu. Not a fun experience. After that, I didn't eat another onion ring for over ten years. That reward was definitely disrupted!

Here is one more example. Over twenty years ago, there was a movie with a talking piglet. I thought he was the cutest little pig I ever saw. It immediately changed my thoughts about ham, bacon, and any other pork product. There was no way I could eat any of it ever again. Eventually, that grew to not eating any meat. And it all started with that cute little piglet. Just in case you're wondering, I do know the piglet didn't really talk.

The HopeandFears.com article [Ref-12] continues, "Start small by giving yourself a new reward for not engaging in the habit and build until you can go for longer periods of time."

After you disrupt the current reward, pick something special and helpful as a new reward for avoiding the old high-speed highway.

Let's go back again to the "sleeping in" example. A new reward for getting up when the alarm sounds is having less stress and more time available before starting your day. But, in the beginning you may need a stronger reward to get started in the right direction. Is there something new you could do with the extra morning time? Or, is there a special event you could plan, like a night out or a trip to the spa?

The longer you avoid using the old highway, the sooner it will lose its highway status in your brain wiring.

Now that you've set up your detour, let's map out your new path to follow.

The man who wants a garden fair,
or small or very big,
With flowers growing here and there,
Must bend his back and dig.

The things are mighty few on earth
That wishes can attain.
Whate'er we want of any worth
We've got to work to gain.

It matters not what goal you seek,
It's secret here reposes:
You've got to dig from week to week
To get Results or Roses.

Edgar A. Guest
from "Results or Roses"

CUE &TRIGGER WORKSHEET

Cue	Behavior	Reward
Current:		
New Alternative:		
Current:		
New Alternative:		
Current:		
New Alternative:		

CHAPTER EIGHT

CREATING A NEW PATH

Every time you are tempted to react in the same old way, ask if you want to be a prisoner of the past or a pioneer of the future. ~Deepak Chopra

Picture yourself standing on the side of a highway. You're looking up at a big orange detour sign with an arrow pointing to your right. When you look that way, you see a large overgrown field, and you feel confused. Why would I leave this nicely paved highway to walk through a field? But in the distance, just beyond the field, you see something interesting.

You think, "What is that?" while you pull out your binoculars. As you adjust the focus, the picture gets clearer; you are looking at your Big Bright Why. All of a sudden, the confusion disappears; and you feel the excitement rising inside. Now you remember why there is a detour, and you know what needs to be done. You are going to forge a new path through this field and get to your Big Bright Why!

During the time it takes to achieve your Big Bright Why, you are going to find yourself in this scenario quite a few times. The people who succeed are those who take the detour more often than they stay on the high-speed highway.

In our analogy, the overgrown field represents what behavioral scientists call the "Intention-Action gap." In their guide, the Behavioral Architects [Ref-15] give us an example, "There is a proven gulf between intending to exercise daily and actually doing it. Most adults know exercise is good for them and would like to do more, yet global studies have shown that between 36% to 55% of people never manage to convert intention into action."

Most of us can relate to that statistic in one way or another. It is when we know what we should be doing but fail to do it. In our analogy, we would stay on the easy high-speed highway instead of creating a new path through the field.

Implementing steps one through six will give you an above-average advantage to overcoming the Intention-Action gap.

We already covered how important it is to change the environment that provides the cue to our unwanted behavior. The environment is equally as important when it comes to setting up a new behavior.

The Behavioral Architects [Ref-15] continue, "This element is an absolutely essential precondition – if the context or surrounding environment is not set up for the desired habit, even the most determined, obstinate characters are going to struggle to even start a new habit, let alone embed it!"

Step Seven of rewiring your brain is for you to set up an accommodating environment to successfully implement your new behavior.

While our old cues and rewards were set up unconsciously, this time we will be deliberately creating them to empower our new path.

An important element of setting up the right environment is that it needs to be "stable and consistent."

"Habits are always triggered by a cue, typically in a context that is stable and consistent in our lives. The cue triggers our memory of doing the same action or routine previously and helps to initiate it again." They continue, "We can be motivated to repeat a behavior if we believe we will reap some sort of reward. It is this element which can fix a behavior in place so it becomes a habit." The Behavior Architects [Ref-15].

After I had disrupted my old cue of eating in front of the TV, my new cue became to consistently sit in my favorite chair in the kitchen when eating. The reward for that behavior was that I enjoyed my meal and felt satisfied after eating. I set up a stable and consistent environment with a cue and a reward without realizing it. How easy was that? Actually, it was very easy.

Do not make things more complicated than they need to be. You are more likely to stick with a new behavior that is easier. Use that to your advantage and then continue to add new behaviors as the previous ones are set in place. You will learn about the time it takes to develop a new habit shortly.

Part of preparing your environment for success is also letting the people in your environment know what you are doing. Having their support can be helpful, but it's not necessary. Remember, this is your Big Bright Why; it is up to you to achieve it. That is the reason your Action Goals are based on behaviors that are within your control.

Another way to help re-enforce a new behavior is by "piggybacking" it onto another behavior. For example, adding exercise into your morning routine could make it easier to adapt than waiting to exercise in the evening. Leave your workout clothes on the bathroom vanity and put them on right after brushing your teeth. Then you get the workout done right away instead of finding excuses for not doing it later in the day. Remember, the simplest way is always the best way.

We now know that consistently repeating a behavior in a stable environment, along with cues and rewards, will lead to creating a new habit. But how long does it take to rewire that path in our brain?

In 2009 researchers at the University College London [Ref-16] conducted a study to find out how long it took a behavior to become a habit. What they found was a range from 18 to 254 days. The median time was 66 days.

The time it takes to create a habit varies with each person and is dependent on the habit being created. However, the most important factor is how consistently the behavior is repeated. I know I have said that before, and I will be saying it again. It is a point worth repeating. Get it? Repetition is a learning tool that works.

Like Thoreau's quote at the beginning of Chapter Six, we do not wear a path through a field by walking across it once. We have to walk across that same area over and over before a path begins to appear.

The time it takes to develop a new path is well worth the effort. That new habit will create the positive changes you want to see in your life.

However, pay attention to the habits you are creating. This process works for both positive and negative behaviors. Watch the actions you are consistently and repeatedly doing.

The same study at University College London [Ref-16] found some encouraging news. Missing a day while in the process of creating a new habit did not affect the outcome of the habit formation. However, missing more than one day in a row did cause a setback with creating the new habit.

Since we're human, we might miss a day here or there while rewiring our brain. It is good to know that all we need to do is get right back on course. There is no time to beat yourself up for missing a day. Just get back to creating your new path right away.

Now we know how to form the paths that will become our new high-speed highways. Next, we'll learn how to stay on those paths long enough to complete the rewiring process.

Beyond myself, somewhere,
I wait for my arrival.

~Octavio Paz
from "The Balcony"

CHAPTER NINE

THE WILL TO BE

Willpower isn't something that gets handed out to some and not to others. It is a skill you can develop through understanding and practice.
~Gillian Riley

Willpower seems to be a mystery for most of us. Why do some people have so much of it while others seem to struggle? Why do people do better with their willpower in the morning but have a problem controlling their behavior toward the end of the day?

From what we have learned so far, it would appear people who have a lot of willpower must have created a high-speed highway, while those who struggle are using smaller roads or paths. That makes sense with the way our brain works. The more we use our willpower, the more neuron space it will occupy in our brain, and the better we will get at using it.

Willpower reminds me of the analogy about what came first, the chicken or the egg. If we had willpower, we could use it more, but what if we don't have the willpower to start?

The basis of willpower is our ability to resist immediate temptations for the delayed reward of reaching a future goal. That doesn't sound very exciting, does it? But, then again, with what we've already learned, there are ways to make this more interesting.

The way we think about willpower affects the amount of willpower we have. Let's see what happens when we change the definition of willpower from the last paragraph to this: *The basis of willpower is our ability to focus on the bigger why of our goal rather than succumbing to irrelevant triggers in our environment.*

The second definition is essentially saying the same thing, but it is worded in a more empowering manner. The focus is on the Big Bright Why instead of the temptation. Remember, what we focus on grows.

What we focus on grows, due in part to the Reticular Activating System (RAS) in our brain [16A]. The RAS receives input from our sensory nerves and determines what information passes onto the thinking part of our brain. It is like a filter that keeps unnecessary stimuli from clogging up our thinking. Our RAS knows what is important to us from where our attention is focused.

A good example of this is when you're thinking of buying a new car and decide on the make and model you want to purchase. Then, the next time you go out, you see that car everywhere. Now that you are focusing on what you want to buy, the RAS begins to allow that stimulus to enter into your thinking. Previously, it would have been filtered out.

That is part of the reason we have such a hard time making changes. When we focus on feeling deprived about giving something up, our RAS continues to let in the stimuli of feeling deprived into our thinking. But if our focus is consistently on our Big Bright Why, our RAS will begin to filter out the feelings of deprivation and allow the new goal-oriented stimuli to enter our thinking.

Carol Dweck, a Professor of Psychology at Stanford University [Ref-17], conducted a study where some participants were told willpower was a limited resource due to its reliance on glucose levels, while other participants were told willpower was unlimited. The study showed that the participants who thought willpower was unlimited performed better than those who thought it wasn't. The group who thought glucose was required to maintain their willpower needed a snack during the study. The results stated, "A nonlimited theory of willpower liberates people from the need for constant glucose boosts to exert self-control successfully."

This study brings us into the mix of a research controversy. Before Dweck's study, researches believed willpower was tied to glucose (among other things) and therefore was limited. That was based on studies by social psychologist Roy Baumeister. [Ref-18] His studies showed that once participants performed an act of willpower, they had less willpower for the following task. Of course, it is all a bit more complicated; but, I'm keeping this simple for us non-researchers.

Even as I write this, the debate continues. However, in a more recent study, Baumeister [Ref-19] shows that people who are motivated perform better, even if they have depleted resources, like being tired. "The most plausible conclusion is that motivation (like cognition and perhaps emotion) can compensate for the reduced ability to self-regulate that ordinarily marks the depleted state." In other words, participants in Baumeister's study were still able to use their willpower even though, according to his beliefs, they had used up their willpower supply. He concluded that the participants' motivation is what made the difference.

Although researches are continuing their studies, I believe both factions have proved something we can all use in our daily lives.

The way we think does affect our results.

Another interesting study was conducted by Dr. Vanessa Patrick, a Bauer Professor of Marketing at the University of Houston [Ref-20]. During the study, some participants were instructed to use the words "I can't" when considering unhealthy food options. The rest of the participants were instructed to use the words "I don't" under the same circumstances.

At the point when the participants thought the study was completed, they were offered a granola bar or chocolate bar before leaving. From the group that had been instructed to say "I can't," 34% chose the granola bar, while 64% of the "I don't" participants chose the granola bar over the chocolate bar. Their results state, "In the current research, we demonstrate an important link between word choice and motivation."

When we say "I can't," we're not accepting the decision as a personal choice. It's like someone told you not to do something. But when we say "I don't," it's a statement of who you are. We have the power to choose. "I don't eat chocolate bars" is a much stronger statement and one that empowers your willpower.

Okay, so now you've seen some evidence of how our thinking controls our actions, and how those actions create our results. Keeping that in mind, how does our self-talk affect our willpower?

A lot of people have that little nagging voice inside that tells them they can't do anything right and can never achieve what they want. That little negative voice repeatedly points out everything that has gone wrong in their life. You get the idea.

Self-criticism is a major roadblock to expanding our willpower highway. This goes right back to Step One, which is believing you can accomplish what you want to achieve.

An article titled "Psychology of Willpower" at the Positive Psychology Program website [Ref-21] says this about self-criticism: "Contrary to common sense, guilt and shame often don't lead to change but to overindulging. Feeling bad makes it harder to resist temptation."

Letting that little voice run rampant in our thoughts weakens our willpower and prevents us from reaching important goals. Every time you say, "I don't have any willpower," you're dooming your chances of having any. What you are actually doing is re-enforcing the wrong high-speed highway.

In an article titled the "Science of Willpower" in the Stanford Medicine Scope Blog [Ref-22], author Lisa Steakley explains, "Research shows that when you scale up to the big want, the biggest why, you automatically have more willpower. You'll look for opportunities to make progress on your goal and be more likely to see how small choices can help you realize your goal."

Use your willpower to stay focused on your Big Bright Why. Doing so will keep you motivated, it will prevent you from listening to negative self-talk, and it will keep you from being distracted by temptations. It is one simple solution to increase your willpower without having to deal with each issue separately.

One of my favorite quotes about willpower is from an article in the Harvard Business Review [Ref-23]. Author Nir Eyal says, "Instead of focusing on willpower, we should look to the power of will."

Next, we'll explore ways to increase the power of your will.

Courage must come from the soul within,
The man must furnish the will to win.

Edgar Guest
from "Equipment"

MINDSET SCIENCE

CHAPTER TEN

ASPIRATIONS

Sight is seeing with the eyes; vision is seeing with the mind. ~Orrin Woodward

Staying focused on your Big Bright Why shouldn't be too much of a mystery if you defined yours correctly. I have heard the strength of our focus being compared to falling in love. When you fall in love, you don't need reminders to keep that relationship in your mind.

That is what we need to do with our Big Bright Why, especially in the beginning when we are first starting to rewire our high-speed highways.

We need to fall in love with our Big Bright Way and stay motivated to do what needs to be done so we get there. The way we do that is by using affirmations and visualization. Studies now show how our brain responds to using these methods and the benefits we can expect to receive from them.

In a study documented in the Oxford Academic [Ref-24], researchers used functional magnetic resonance imaging (fMRI) to see what areas of the brain were affected while participants said different types of self-affirmations. They found the reward centers of the brain were most affected by the affirmations. And, that future-oriented affirmations were stronger than affirmations related to past events. The researchers explain, "Affirmations can decrease stress, increase well-being, improve academic performance and make people more open to behavior change."

In the past, affirmations were an easy target for late night comedians. But now, studies show the true benefit of what a lot of us have known for years: affirmations do help to change behavior.

In an article in Psychology Today [Ref-25] titled "Happy Brain, Happy Life," the authors state, "Repetitive mental activity can affect changes in your brain's structure, wiring, and capabilities." We're going to use affirmations as a tool for our new wiring efforts.

Step Eight of rewiring your brain is for you to create two affirmations to repeat consistently every day.

The reason we're starting with two affirmations and not more is to keep this process easier to implement.

Here are the guidelines to follow:

- Affirmations should be in a first-person narrative. (Example: *I am . . .*)
- Affirmations should be stated in the present tense. (Example: *I am happy*. Do not use the future tense: *I will be happy*.)
- Affirmations should be positive in nature and wording. (Example: *Every day I get healthier and more fit.*)

Your first affirmation will be a Declaration Statement. It should be something that makes you feel empowered. My favorite is: *I am Worthy, Deserving, Powerful, Capable, and Confident!* Whenever I repeat this affirmation, I say it with intensity. It's a DECLARATION; this is not the time to be timid. Put feeling into the words and start laying that new path with conviction.

The second affirmation will be a Rewiring Statement. It should be a statement that helps to re-enforce the new behaviors you are rewiring into your brain. This refers to the Action Goals you created at Step Four.

Let's use Jennifer as our example again. To reach her Big Bright Why, she determined that she had to start saving at least $300 every week.

Jennifer's Rewiring Affirmation could look like this: *I easily save $300 every week, and it feels great.*

Once a rewiring affirmation has become a high-speed highway, you can create a new one to replace the old one. The way you know when an affirmation has become part of a high-speed highway is by observing your behaviors and asking, "Has this action become a habit?" If that action is now a behavior that happens without thinking about it, you are ready to move onto a new affirmation.

Affirmation Examples

- I am healthy, energetic, and optimistic.
- I am decisive, determined, disciplined, and dynamic!
- My confidence, self-esteem, and inner wisdom increase every day.
- I trust my ability to do what needs to be done every day.
- I grow more confident and stronger every day.
- I make wise decisions and take immediate action.
- Every decision I make brings me closer to my goals.
- I learn and adapt from every situation I encounter.

- I have the strength and power to achieve my goals.
- I am positive and persistent.

As you write your affirmations, use words and phrases that inspire, motivate, and empower you. If you do not believe a statement, change it slightly to include wording that works for you. The following affirmations are good examples of changing words to eliminate conflicts with your current thinking.

- *I am confident.* Can be changed to *My confidence increases every day*.
- *I am positive.* Can be changed to *I find things to be grateful for every day*.

Remember, we want the reward center of our brain to light up whenever we repeat them.

Once you have your affirmations ready, it's time to start implementing them into your day. I'm a

121

firm believer that everyone has to find what works best for themselves. Repeating each affirmation between five and ten times in a row at least three times a day is what worked for me. Research participants dedicated from five to fifteen minutes per day for self-affirmation during their studies [Ref-25a] and [Ref-25b]. Experimenting will teach you what your ideal number of repetitions is.

Keep your affirmations written on an index card or saved as your phone wallpaper. Always keep them in an easy-to-see spot. Minimally, repeat them when you first wake-up, mid-day, and before going to sleep at night. The more you repeat them, the faster they will embed into your wiring and create your new highway.

To super-charge your start-up, try the following tip. Before going to sleep at night, write out your affirmation twenty times and say it aloud as you write. Doing this engages multiple areas of the brain. You're actively writing the words, you see what you've written, you're saying the words, and hearing the words you're speaking. That's a lot of activity toward creating your new highway.

Psychologists call this process the "generation effect." Studies show that people who wrote out the information they were learning significantly improved their memory. This was not typing information into a computer; it was actually writing the information on paper [Ref-26].

Now we'll move onto using visualization as another method of rewiring your high-speed highway.

In an article in Psychology Today [Ref-27] titled "To Affirm or Not Affirm," author Leena S. Guptha explains, "The subconscious mind cannot differentiate between negative and positive, or between what is real and imagined." Remember the piano-playing study in Chapter Four? The group that visualized playing the piano had the same increase in neurons as the group that actually played the piano. Their brain did not differentiate the real from the vividly imagined.

Elliot T. Berkman, Ph.D. and colleagues [Ref-28] explain,

> "Visualizing something produces brain activation that is consistent with actually engaging in that action. . . When we see somebody acting (visualizing) the motor system in our brain mimics that action so that when we try to do it, those brain regions have already had some practice."

Step Nine of rewiring your brain is for you to create visualization "scenes" of yourself completing your Action Goals.

When you create a visualization scene, you are the writer, director, and actor. Here are guidelines to follow:

- Use as many of your senses as possible.
- Add positive emotional feelings.
- Use vivid details to describe the scene.

Your visualization movie will serve to strengthen your Action Goals behavior. Curtin University [Ref-29] in Western Australia published a research article showing healthy behaviors were more easily adapted when participants visualized themselves doing the activity or task first.

Let's consider our example with Jennifer. One of her Action Goals was to save $300 every week. She can develop a scene of herself writing out a deposit slip for $300 and depositing it at her bank. Jennifer's vivid scene can include what she's wearing, what the weather is like, and what she sees as she walks up to the bank. She can smell the flowers along the sidewalk and then hear her heels clicking on the marble floor as she enters the lobby. The teller smiles as Jennifer makes her deposit. And as she leaves the bank, she can feel the emotions of being happy and excited about making another deposit as she looks at her increasing balance.

Studies are showing that visualizing the process of reaching our goals increases the progress to achieving the goal. When you visualize yourself completing a SMART Action Goal, you feel more in control and are willing to complete the action because it already feels like it is part of your normal routine. Your brain has already started the wiring process before you've even engaged in the behavior. Sheffield Hallam University [Ref-30], National Center for Biotechnology Information, U.S. National Library of Medicine [Ref-31], and Social Psychological and Personality Science [Ref-32].

Now I have to share some shocking information. This information goes against the grain of everything I've believed for decades. It comes from the same studies mentioned in the previous paragraph that show visualizing the process of reaching a goal leads to more success. Their studies also showed that visualizing your Big Bright Why goal as already completed did not add any value toward achieving that outcome. And, the Social Psychological and Personality Science study [Ref-32] actually said doing so predicted, "Greater distress, dissatisfaction, and dysfunction."

The studies showed that people who visualized their Big Bright Why as being completed were less motivated to take the actions necessary to reach it, while those who visualized the *process of achieving* their Action Goals became more motivated to do what needed to be done to reach their end goal, their Big Bright Why.

The group who visualized their Big Bright Why as completed were so content with their visualization that they didn't feel the need to take action toward achieving that goal. The researchers did point out that visualizing the completed goal was a good way to combat stressful thinking, but it did nothing to motivate behavior changes.

This seems like a subtle change to what I had believed; but, it is a powerful change. One that makes the difference between reaching our Big

Bright Why or just seeing it in our heads until we die. Sorry for the bluntness.

Learning this caused me distress. But on a deeper level, it actually felt like I found the missing piece of a puzzle. I had always visualized myself thin, fit, and happy; but I could never reach that outcome. Was visualizing my goal as already completed the reason I wasn't able to reach my weight loss goals for three decades? Was that the reason why I gave up, weighed 394 pounds, and was in a wheelchair, unable to breathe?

The more I thought about this, the more I realized that this time I had accidentally been pushed into visualizing my Action Goals instead of visualizing my Big Bright Why goal.

When I started the process to lose weight (this last time), I didn't think I had a future. I just jumped through each hoop, one Action Goal at a time.

Frankly, I was too busy trying to survive and couldn't think any further than that.

My "why" was to lose weight so I could breathe and hopefully walk again. It was a slow, steady process. But, thankfully, I was finally able to reach my elusive weight loss goal. I just took it one moment at a time until I could see there was going to be a brighter future. Once again, I had stumbled upon what worked before knowing why it did.

After thinking about this, I started to feel betrayed by the self-help industry. How could they not know about these studies? Did they even care? Were they so out of touch with normal people that they just all repeated the same blather?

I felt ashamed for having bought into this belief that hurts more than it helps. I felt sad about all the time and money wasted over the years.

Then I started to feel empowered. I had to share this new-found information with as many people as I could. That is why this book isn't just about my story. This is not my secret recipe for success. It's a book with proven research to support what works.

Self-help is a $9.9 billion industry. Business Wire [Ref-33]. What I'm about to say may seem controversial, but it needs to be said. Some people in the self-help industry seem disingenuous. They mislead people who sincerely want to improve their lives into spending thousands of dollars on programs that don't work. We regular folks just keep fighting to change our lives with that same information that's been proven not to work.

Don't get me wrong. I believe people should be compensated for the value they bring to others. But misleading people with information that's proven not to work doesn't bring value to anyone. And it is more than a disservice to people who really want and need to change their lives.

There is a fine line between motivation and discouragement. It's a hard line to see, but one that affects us more than we know. This was my wake-up call, and I hope it is yours as well.

Change can happen. And it's appropriate to be open to new researched-backed information. But be discerning about unsubstantiated claims thrown around by gurus. Testimonials on a website or sales page don't prove anything. It's all part of a marketing strategy.

And, in case anyone was wondering, yes, I know that, technically, writing this book is considered part of the Self-Help industry. However, this book is backed with research because I am not a guru. I'm a regular person who discovered what worked. Then I wanted to find out why it worked and share my discoveries with others.

Our Big Bright Why is still very important to our goal achievement process. We need to know where we're going in order to get there. But, the way we get there is by visualizing our Action Goals. Using both the Big Bright Why and our Action Goals together give us the complete road map. We know where we're going and which roads to take to get there.

Next, we'll learn the truth about positive thinking. Does research show that it really works?

Let us, then, be up and doing,
With a heart for any fate;
Still achieving, still pursuing,
Learn to labor and to wait.

Henry Wadsworth Longfellow
from "A Psalm of Life"

MINDSET SCIENCE

CHAPTER ELEVEN

LOOKING FOR SOLUTIONS

Problems cannot be solved by the same level of thinking that created them. ~Albert Einstein

In previous chapters, we have learned how our thinking affects our behaviors, which affect our actions, which create the results we see in our lives. So, how does positive thinking fit into our rewiring process?

There seems to be a general misunderstanding that positive thinking is akin to being naive. But having a positive mindset is not ignoring negative circumstances and challenges; it's having a mindset that looks for solutions to obstacles instead of dwelling on the negative consequences.

Remember, self-talk is a big part of our mindset. We can be our worst critic or our biggest cheerleader. And, we don't need to be a neuroscientist to know which one is better at improving our outlook on life.

In a study in National Center for Biotechnology Information, U.S. National Library of Medicine [Ref-34], researches explain, "A large and growing literature indicates that people who dispositionally hold positive expectations for the future respond to difficulty and adversity in more adaptive ways than people who hold negative expectations."

The key word in the above quote is "adaptive." A positive mindset allows us to be open to making changes when they are needed—just like Einstein's quote at the beginning of this chapter. The same thinking that got us to where we are will not take us to where we want to go. Life is a journey of learning and adapting. To reach our goals, we need to learn from our mistakes and challenges. But, we also need to change our behavior to move beyond those circumstances.

People with a negative mindset have a harder time making the necessary behavior changes to move beyond their current circumstances. They see obstacles and challenges as something that's being inflicted upon them. And they rarely have the motivation to learn, adapt, and move forward from their problems. Their lives become a vicious cycle of frustration and disappointment. But it doesn't have to be that way.

Having a positive mindset allows you to overcome challenges easier. It's not that life is filled with rainbows and unicorns. But by being positive, you become proactive when problems arise instead of being overwhelmed by them. Researchers in an Optimism study [Ref-35] state, "People who are confident about eventual success continue trying, even when the going is hard. People who are doubtful try to escape the adversity by wishful thinking . . ."

Wishful thinking doesn't have to be a far-off fantasy. It can be as simple as thinking *If this circumstance wasn't in my way, I might be able to do this*. People with a negative mindset will find all sorts of reasons why they can't do something instead of finding the "how" to overcome their challenges.

Let's take a look at some of the emotions that accompany these two mindsets. We've all probably felt these at some point during our lives.

A negative mindset is accompanied by anger, sadness, guilt, worry, hopelessness, fear, anxiety, hate, self-loathing, and frustration (to name a few). Doesn't sound very appealing, does it?

A positive mindset is accompanied by happiness, joy, gratitude, confidence, enthusiasm, satisfaction, love, hope, well-being, pride, and others. Now, that sounds more inviting.

I like the analogy of negative thoughts being like weeds that need to be pulled from the soil of our minds. The last thing we want to do is nurture a weed when we could be growing a beautiful flower. But, if we don't pull the weeds out, they will overtake the whole garden. When that happens, we are left with a negative mindset. Always remember, what we focus on grows. Whether the thought is positive or negative, it will grow.

In the article "Pay Attention" [Ref-36], Rick Hanson, Ph.D. explains,

> "Because of what's called "experience-dependent neuroplasticity," whatever you hold in attention has a special power to change your brain. Attention is like a combination spotlight and vacuum cleaner, it illuminates what it rests upon and then sucks it into your brain – and yourself."

That's a scary thought when you think about it that way. Our focus is powerful, and most of the time we just tag along for the ride without realizing we could be in the driver's seat.

Here is an example of what the word "no" does to the brain:

> "If I were to put you into an fMRI scanner—a huge donut-shaped magnet that can take a video of the neural changes happening in your brain—and flash the word "NO" for less than one second, you'd see a sudden release of dozens of stress-producing hormones and neurotransmitters. These chemicals immediately interrupt the normal functioning of your brain, impairing logic, reason, language processing, and communication." Psychology

Today [Ref-37] Andrew Newberg, M.D. and Mark Waldman.

I seriously hope you can now see how detrimental a negative mindset can be to your life and how having a positive mindset can change your reality. Are you ready to alter your thinking and create positive changes that will guide you to your Big Bright Why?

Jeffrey M. Schwartz, M.D. [Ref-38] is a leading psychiatrist and researcher in the field of neuroplasticity. He developed a therapy which he named "Self-Directed Neuroplasticity." This well-researched therapy has documented the rewiring of his patient's brains after they had consciously changed their thought patterns.

Dr. Schwartz [Ref-39] used his Self-Directed Neuroplasticity therapy with OCD patients. They were instructed to monitor their thinking;

and, whenever they experienced an obsessive thought, they were to think of a different thought that Dr. Schwartz had given them to substitute. After ten weeks of therapy, 12 out of 18 patients' brain scans showed significant improvement. And the improvements occurred in the same areas of the brain that effective medications for OCD work. The brain scans proved the patients had changed their brain by controlling their thoughts.

Step Ten of rewiring your brain is for you to become mindful of your negative thoughts and change them into positive thoughts.

There are four steps to the process of Self-Directed Neuroplasticity [Ref-40].

1. **Relabel**: This is where you start to pay attention to your thoughts. When you become aware of a negative thought or

feeling, you label it with a description. For example, *That's just an A.N.T.* (An automatic negative thought.)

2. **Reframe**: This is where you take the label from the first step and change your perception of it. Realize that this is a deceptive message that you don't have to believe. For example, ask yourself, "Is something really wrong or is this a weed*?*" Then tell yourself, *it's time to pull the weeds.*

3. **Refocus**: This is where you change your focus away from the negative thought, even while you're still experiencing the negative feelings. Bring your focus back to the present moment and consciously do something more constructive. This helps to distract your brain from continuing to contemplate on the negative thought [Ref-

40]. "It's through the refocusing of your attention that the brain gets rewired." This would also be a good time to use a positive affirmation to replace the negative thought. For example: *I'm taking control over my thoughts. I'm feeling more hopeful every day.*

4. **Revalue**: This is where [Ref-40], "You begin to see thoughts, urges, and impulses for what they are: sensations caused by deceptive brain messages that don't benefit you." You'll realize that it is no longer necessary to believe and act on every thought that crosses your mind.

Once again, the only way this process works is by consistently and repeatedly cutting off the negative thought instead of letting it fester. Using Self-Directed Neuroplasticity sporadically will not be enough to make permanent changes. Though, any time you use this process, it will help end the negative emotions accompanying that thought at that moment in time.

Changing a negative mindset does not happen overnight. It takes consistent effort on your part. But the more you do it, the easier it will become. Keep the momentum moving forward, and you will change the wiring of your brain. And when that happens, it will be just like riding a bicycle again.

Use the following worksheet for developing the Refocus step. Write your negative thought in the first column and the exact opposite thought in the next. You can use that new positive thought for rewiring your new highway.

Once you become aware of your negative thinking, you'll most likely discover distinct patterns. Certain circumstances may trigger a negative thought which leads you to an undesired behavior.

Next, we'll learn ways to prepare in advance for the patterns you find on your current high-speed highways.

> *I know not whence I came,*
> *I know not whither I go;*
> *But the fact stands clear that I am here*
> *In this world of pleasure and woe.*
> *And out of the mist and murk*
> *Another truth shines plain –*
> *It is my power each day and hour*
> *To add to its joy or its pain.*
> Ella Wheeler Wilcox
> from "I Am"

NEGATIVE AND POSITIVE THOUGHTS

Negative Thought	New Positive Thought

CHAPTER TWELVE

PREPARE TO WIN

You must weed your mind as you would weed your garden. ~Astrid Alauda

In the last chapter, we learned how to reroute a negative thought once you become aware of it. Now we're going to become proactive by learning how to weed the garden in advance.

There is a lot of self-reflection during the process of rewiring your brain. And no doubt, you'll find patterns of negativity within your thinking. After all, we are human. But that's not an excuse to continue living a life that doesn't fulfill us.

One of the best ways to prepare for success while creating your new highways is by creating a plan to deal with your negative thoughts and behaviors. Being prepared helps you move from not knowing how to deal with challenges to feeling more confident overcoming them.

Just like the "cues" we discussed in Chapter Seven, we have triggers that set off negative thoughts. Like our habits, these thoughts set up an automatic response of emotions and behavior. When we know what our triggers are, we can develop a plan to meet those challenges head on instead of suffering from their consequences.

These triggers can be emotional or situational. The difference is emotional triggers are fueled by feelings while situational triggers are fueled by certain people, places, or events.

Let's use Jennifer as an example again. Jennifer works in a chaotic environment. After having a difficult day, she goes home feeling depleted and stressed. That's when she goes online for some "shopping therapy." She spends hours looking for and buying things she never realized she needed until that exact moment. She enjoys the shopping spree while it lasts; but, afterward, she feels guilty and disappointed with herself. She could cancel the orders but never does.

Logically, Jennifer just added more negative feelings to an already stressful situation. Shopping didn't help; it actually made things worse. But Jennifer doesn't look at it that way. It's a pattern she has had for a long time, and she hasn't even thought about changing it.

That's an example of an emotional trigger. Jennifer's feelings triggered the response of wanting to buy something, and the rest became history.

But now, the difference is Jennifer has discovered her Big Bright Why. She knows going on a shopping spree every time she feels stressed will hinder her from reaching her goal. She has just become consciously aware of her emotional trigger and the results.

Knowing stress causes her to spend money, she can develop an alternative behavior to replace it. Even though she cannot control the events of a day at work, she can control how she reacts to it.

Jennifer decides that the next time she has a bad day at work, she will not go directly home. Instead, she'll meet up with a friend or go to the gym for a dance class. Whatever she does will not revolve around any kind of shopping.

By not going straight home after a stressful day at work, Jennifer will disrupt her current emotionally-triggered behavior. She's giving herself time to decompress and avoid the pattern of a stressed-induced shopping spree. And she won't have to feel guilty and disappointed with herself for spending money that should have been saved. That's a win-win.

Now let's look at a situational trigger.

Jennifer and a few friends go to a brand name outlet mall every month. They love finding a good deal, and it's always a fun time when they get together.

Jennifer enjoys these days out but knows that she'll spend way too much money. She just can't pass up a great deal.

Jennifer knows the shopping trip conflicts with her Action Goal of saving money for her Big Bright Why. But she doesn't want to miss a special time with her friends, and she doesn't want to be tempted by shopping. She needs to develop an alternative plan.

She talks with her friends, and they all decide to visit the zoo instead. And, every month they'll get together to do something that does not revolve around shopping. Now Jennifer can see how switching the destination of their outing will help her to get closer to her Big Bright Why without missing out on the fun of spending time with friends.

Again, this is a simple process for making changes easier. Just anticipate where your normal triggers conflict with your new goals, then plan ahead. We do not need to be held captive by behaviors that lead us further away from our goals. You can pull the weeds before they get too big to handle.

Use the following worksheets to help develop your plan. Start by defining the emotion or situation that is the trigger and write the negative behavior underneath. Then in the next column, write the positive behavior you will do instead.

Next, we'll review our rewiring steps, and I'll share some closing thoughts.

My turn shall also come:
I sense the spreading of a wing.

~Osip Mandelstam
from "The Selected Poems"

EMOTIONAL TRIGGER WORKSHEET

NEGATIVE BEHAVIOR	POSITIVE BEHAVIOR
Emotion:	
Emotion:	
Emotion:	
Emotion:	
Emotion:	
Emotion:	
Emotion:	
Emotion:	

SITUATIONAL TRIGGER WORKSHEET

NEGATIVE BEHAVIOR	POSITIVE BEHAVIOR
Situation:	
Situation:	
Situation:	
Situation:	
Situation:	
Situation:	
Situation:	
Situation:	

CONCLUSION

THE GREAT ESCAPE

If you can change your mind, you can change your life. ~William James

Life sure is an interesting ride. Time passes whether we use it wisely or not. I spent too many years wasting my precious time. Thankfully, I was given a second opportunity to make things better. I hope that by writing this book I can encourage you to use your time better than I did.

Our magnificent brain is ready and willing to do the work if we let it know what's important.

Without our conscious direction, our brain will keep getting better at doing what it's been doing. Now you know change is possible. It's not some pie-in-the-sky platitude. There's research to prove it.

Will it be easy? Probably not. But anything worth achieving requires us to become more than we've been before. Will the results be worth it? YES, they definitely will!

I stumbled upon these principles not realizing what made them work. And ever since, my life has changed for the better in every way possible. Not only did I lose 224 pounds, but I also achieved my lifelong dreams of becoming an author and helping others. These principals work, whether we're aware of them or not. I'm living proof of that.

Let's review our 10 Steps for rewiring your thinking and creating your new high-speed highways.

Step One: *Open the door to believing change is possible for yourself.* You need to have a belief so strong that you <u>expect</u> to reach your goal. No more trying; this time you're doing it!

Step Two: *Find your Big Bright Why.* Discovering your "why" gives meaning and purpose to your goals. Having a Big Bright Why fuels your motivation to stay on course and overcome challenges.

Step Three: *Choose a negative habit to reroute.* Our current habits were formed unconsciously, and those behaviors have become automatic. Now, we have to make a conscious effort to disengage the negative behaviors.

Step Four: *Choose a positive habit to replace the negative habit you picked at Step Three.* It's easier to replace a negative habit with a positive habit than trying to stop an old behavior "cold turkey." Choosing a new habit makes you more productive toward reaching your goals and helps to make the rerouting process easier.

Step Five: *Identify the cue and routine of the habit you chose to reroute and disrupt them.* Every habit has a cue that triggers the routine of a habitual behavior. By disrupting the process, you give yourself an opportunity to replace that behavior with a new one.

Step Six: *Identify the reward you receive from the habit you chose to reroute and disrupt it.* Removing the reward from a negative habit makes it easier to disengage. And the reverse is true, as well. You can anchor a new habit by setting up a reward for following through with that positive behavior.

Step Seven: *Set up an accommodating environment to successfully implement your new behavior.* Studies show this is a "must have" when creating new positive habits. Trying to develop a new behavior in an environment filled with temptations and distractions is setting yourself up to fail.

Step Eight: *Create two affirmations to repeat consistently every day.* Consistently repeating affirmations helps to rewire the circuitry of the brain. You can choose affirmations that help to create your new habits, and you can choose affirmations that strengthen areas of weakness in your perceptions.

Step Nine: *Create visualization scenes of yourself completing your Action Goals.* Studies show that visualizing the process of achieving your Big Bright Why is more motivating than visualizing the ideal outcome of your goal. Visualizing your Action Goals helps to complete the actions necessary for reaching your Big Bright Why.

Step Ten: *Become mindful of your negative thoughts and change them into positive thoughts. Pull the weeds!* People with a positive mindset are more successful at reaching their goals because they overcome obstacles instead of being overwhelmed by them. Pulling the weeds of negative thinking helps you to stay on course and not be distracted during the process of achieving your Big Bright Why.

These ten steps can change your life if you apply what you've learned. I hope you've found the real meaning behind these words and that you can see the possibilities of what you are capable of accomplishing. Get into the driver's seat and create those new high-speed highways. Find your WILL and get it done.

You now have the escape plan. Set yourself free and create the path to becoming the person you've always wanted to BE.

Rapidly, merrily,
Life's sunny hours flit by,
Gratefully, cheerily,
Enjoy them as they fly!

Charlotte Bronte
from "Life"

Connect with Beth at the following Links:

Website: https://BethBianca.com/

Facebook:
https://www.facebook.com/BethBianca.Author/

Receive notifications of new releases, special offers, and motivation tips.

Text the word **LIVING** to **444999**

Download PDF versions of the worksheets included in this book here:

https://BigBrightWhy.com/worksheets/

BIBLIOGRAPHY

[Ref-1]
https://www.wtcmhmr.org/poc/view_index.php
?idx=119&d=1&w=1&e=41061
[Ref-2]
https://brainworksneurotherapy.com/what-
neuroplasticity
[Ref-3]
https://www.psychologytoday.com/us/blog/use-
your-mind-change-your-brain/201106/you-are-
not-your-brain
[Ref-4]
https://www.psychologytoday.com/us/blog/use-
your-mind-change-your-brain/201106/you-are-
not-your-brain
[Ref-5]
http://content.time.com/time/magazine/article/0,
9171,1580438,00.html
[Ref-6]
https://www.researchgate.net/publication/31854
2415_The_Neuroscience_of_Goals_and_Behav
ior_Change

[Ref-7]
https://www.researchgate.net/publication/28002
2285_AIM_An_Integrative_Model_of_Goal_P
ursuit
[Ref-8]
http://www.pnas.org/content/111/30/10990
[Ref-9]
https://hbr.org/2016/03/how-to-build-a-culture-
of-originality
[Ref-10]
https://mentalhealthdaily.com/2015/02/20/self-
directed-neuroplasticity-consciously-changing-
your-brain-function/
[Ref-11]
https://www.sciencedaily.com/releases/2014/08/
140808111931.htm
[Ref-12]
http://www.hopesandfears.com/hopes/now/ques
tion/216479-how-long-does-it-really-take-to-
break-a-habit
[Ref-13]
https://www.psychologytoday.com/us/blog/the-
truisms-wellness/201610/the-science-
accomplishing-your-goals
[Ref-14]
http://www.spsp.org/news-center/press-
releases/resolution-habits

[Ref-15]
https://www.thebearchitects.com/assets/uploads
/TBA_Warc_How_to_use_behavioural_science
_to_build_habits.pdf
[Ref-16]
https://centrespringmd.com/docs/How%20Habit
s%20are%20Formed.pdf
[16A]
http://www.ascd.org/ASCD/pdf/journals/ed_lea
d/el200912_willis.pdf
[Ref-17]
http://www.pnas.org/content/110/37/14837.full
#F1
[Ref-18]
https://www.ncbi.nlm.nih.gov/pubmed/9523419
[Ref-19]
http://assets.csom.umn.edu/assets/90559.pdf
[Ref-20]
https://www.bauer.uh.edu/vpatrick/docs/dontver
suscant.pdf
[Ref-21]
https://positivepsychologyprogram.com/psychol
ogy-of-willpower/
[Ref-22]
https://scopeblog.stanford.edu/2011/12/29/a-
conversation-about-the-science-of-willpower/

[Ref-23]
https://hbr.org/2016/11/have-we-been-thinking-about-willpower-the-wrong-way-for-30-years
[Ref-24]
https://academic.oup.com/scan/article/11/4/621/2375054
[Ref-25]
https://www.psychologytoday.com/us/blog/prime-your-gray-cells/201108/happy-brain-happy-life
[Ref-25a]
https://www.ncbi.nlm.nih.gov/pubmed/21813799
[Ref-25b]
https://www.psychologicalscience.org/news/releases/self-affirmation-enhances-performance-makes-us-receptive-to-our-mistakes.html
[Ref-26]
https://www.ncbi.nlm.nih.gov/pmc/articles/PMC3556209/
[Ref-27]
https://www.psychologytoday.com/us/blog/embodied-wellness/201704/affirm-or-not-affirm
[Ref-28]
https://www.researchgate.net/publication/280101902_A_social_neuroscience_approach_to_goal_setting_for_coaches

[Ref-29]
https://news.curtin.edu.au/media-releases/new-research-finds-mind-matter-key-healthy-lifestyle/
[Ref-30]
http://shura.shu.ac.uk/5075/
[Ref-31]
https://www.ncbi.nlm.nih.gov/pubmed/9572006
[Ref-32]
https://psych.nyu.edu/oettingen/Duckworth_Kir by_Gollwitzer_Oettingen_2013_SPPS.pdf
[Ref-33]
https://www.businesswire.com/news/home/201 80302005568/en/U.S.-Market-Improvement-Products-Services---ResearchAndMarkets.com
[Ref-34]
https://www.ncbi.nlm.nih.gov/pmc/articles/PM C4161121/
[Ref-35]
https://www.ncbi.nlm.nih.gov/pmc/articles/PM C4161121/
[Ref-36]
http://www.rickhanson.net/pay-attention/
[Ref-37]
https://www.psychologytoday.com/us/experts/a ndrew-newberg-md-and-mark-waldman

Ref-38]
http://discovermagazine.com/2013/nov/14-
defense-free-will
[Ref-39]
http://content.time.com/time/magazine/article/0,
9171,1580438,00.html
[Ref-40]
https://www.thebestbrainpossible.com/four-
steps-to-take-control-of-your-mind-and-change-
your-brain/

ABOUT THE AUTHOR

Beth Bianca spent thirty years trying to change her negative habits. She read the self-development gurus' books and tried their advice. But she always went back to her old behaviors. After giving up for years, Beth had a rude awakening. That life-threatening event taught her the important lessons missing from the gurus' books.

Now, Beth is devoted to helping people discover their ability to escape negative behaviors so that they can become who they CHOOSE TO BE, without having to struggle.

Beth Bianca is the author of five books, a certified coach, and a Huffington Post contributor.